HAPPE Press A Division of HAPPE Programs, Inc.
183 Saint Paul Street
Rochester, New York 14604
1-800-784-2773

© 1997 by Jessie M. James.

All rights reserved. Printed in the United States of America. No part of this publication may be reproduced, stored in a retrieval system, or transmitted in any form or by any means, electronic, mechanical, photocopying, recording, or otherwise, without prior written permission of the publisher.

ISBN 1-57582-028-5

A Journey of Self-Discovery

Common Sense: Not So Common

Honesty

Self-Esteem

Spirituality

Fulfillment

Jessie M. James
COMMON SENSE ADVISOR

Acknowledgments

Through a myriad of personal experiences, observations, teaching tasks, counseling sessions, workshop presentations and speaking engagements, I have finally decided to write. There are so many people who have encouraged this endeavor, such as, Maxine Carey, a friend and student, and Rev. Dr. Charles Thurman, my mentor and spiritual advisor. In addition, I want to thank my family: special thanks to Shirley Green for her dramatics; Eddie Green for "telling it like it is"; Willie Green for having a sense of humor; Gladys and Emory Green for wisdom, insights and a listening ear; Pearlie Trotter, my sister, for challenging my blockages and my thoughts; "Mother" Maggie Black for her continual support. Thanks also go to: Joan Lane, Evelyn HosPedales, the Aenon Baptist Missionary Church, Pastor James L. Cherry, Sr. and the Rochester Area Great Lakes Women's Association.

Lastly, I want to thank the many participants and students of my classes and workshops who also helped and inspired this process. To all those who granted me interviews, "thank you". Special thanks to typist Brenda LeGree, who put in many long hours typing the various stages of this manuscript and for her cheerfulness and constant enthusiasm, and to the friends who read and criticized portions of the manuscript in progress, providing insight, new ideas and clarification as I struggled through my endeavor. A heartfelt thanks to Judith Baker, Ruth Brooks-Ward, Pearlie E. Ragland, Denise Kirby and Shirley Allen.

Table of Contents

Acknowledgements v
Dedication ix
Preface xi
Introduction 1
Overview of Steps to Common Sense Therapy 5
Step One - Joining and Engaging 11
Step Two - Information Gathering 15
Step Three - Identifying and Analyzing 21
Step Four - Acceptance or Refocusing 29
Step Five - Strategies and Goals 37
Step Six - Evaluation 43
Love Lifted Me - Conclusion 47
Getting to Know Me 51
Suggested Readings 65
Seminar Information 67
Getting to Know Jessie 69
Contact information 71

Dedication

In memoriam to
My parents: Wonder Clair, Marion and Marietta Green

To My Family
Derrick James, Sr., Derrick James, Jr., Theresa B. James, Mary G. James, Darryl L. James and Jessica M. James

To My Sisters and Brothers
Eddie Green, Emory and Gladys Green, Willie Lee and Dorothy Green, Pearlie M. and Alexander Trotter, Shirley A. Green-Bryant, Rev. Roosevelt and Betty Green, and Edna Lee and Wallace Jones

Preface

This workbook has been designed and laid out for use by several audiences. It is intended for people:

- Nurtured in Christian tradition who have not experienced groups or experiments in nonverbal communication.
- Who want to explore its usefulness for the religious community and the shaping of their spiritual life.
- Who may have participated in groups but who have not yet learned to assess how that experience relates to their understanding of self-disclosure, honesty, self-esteem, spirituality, fulfillment and communication.
- Whose lives have been shaped by group experiences but who do not think of themselves in a spiritual way.

I am not an expert and this is not a technical book for experts in this field. This book is about taking care of and feeling better about yourself.

This book grew out of my research, my personal and professional experiences, and my passion for the subject. It is personal and, in some places, prejudiced opinion.

This is a self-help, "how to" book, not a book for mental health. Each person is unique, each situation is different. Try to tap into your own healing process, which may include seeking professional help, attending support groups and calling on a power greater than yourself.

In the Bible, the Book of Proverbs teaches that there is a divine wisdom given to man and woman by God, but there is also a divinely given human wisdom, or common sense, and both must play a part in daily life. Human wisdom is fine and necessary. No matter how skilled a person might be, without humility and a willingness to learn from God, he or she will inevitably go astray.

Sessions may range in time from three hours in an afternoon or evening to intensive weekend workshops.

The hoped for result is improved learning about oneself, a mixture of techniques and resources, small group discussion, behavior psychology, human relations, leadership training, meditation, "tuning" in to problems and needs.

Introduction

Growing up in a home with loving Christian parents, I had relatively normal childhood experiences and I knew that I was somebody. However, when I married, I was faced with circumstances which caused me to fear and doubt myself.

Blinded by love, my husband and I were unable to see the differences in our personalities, our style and approach to communication which would be problematic during the years that we raised our children and grandchildren. This caused great anxiety, frustration and pain for both of us.

It wasn't until the 1960's that I began to seek help. It was then that I learned to use spiritual exercises, meditation, support groups and prayer on a regular basis. During these times, I became conscious of revelations and insights which proved to be very helpful in my personal journey to self-discovery. Many trusted friends were beneficial in helping me to honestly see myself in a loving and capable way.

As I gained insight into the source of my feelings, they gradually began to lose their hold on me. I can now share even my most embarrassing secrets with trusted people, secrets that, once, I would have kept to myself. I found that honest sharing is the key to healing.

The truth will set you free.

Spirituality is about relationships, those we have with ourselves, with others and with the universe. It is subtle and powerful. It is highly useful. Spirituality is indescribable, inclusive, supportive and healing. It is not organized religion. It is fulfilling. Spirituality transcends our intellect and logic. It is an ongoing process.

Spirituality is truth!

Common Sense Therapy (CST)

Common Sense Therapy seeks to be compassionate and encouraging, not to belittle, judge or point an accusatory finger. It has a practical understanding of people and problems, that "we are our brothers' and sisters' keepers". It is sensitive and compassionate. This is what God demands of us all, even in the area of counseling. "be ye all of one mind, having compassion, one of another, love as brethren, be pitiful, be courteous..." (I Peter 3:8)

People who do not adapt well to changing situations are at greater risk of losing their intellectual abilities. For example, when a loved one dies or a son leaves home without saying good-bye, these are unavoidable changes. We can mourn the changes and gradually we will heal. Or, we can go into a deep depression or anxiety, blaming others or ourselves for the situation.

It is time to move, to be flexible, to grow and to change. Denial can keep us from changing. In spite of life's constant flux, many of us become so rigidly attached to familiar things that our lives seem more like stagnant ponds. Some of us live life in a fixed, well-defined mode and suffer when any change or interference alters our circumstances. Our energies are spent resisting change in an effort to protect what we think we have.

The ability to change and the willingness to change are important factors in living a satisfactory and fulfilling life.

"Where there is no vision, the people perish."

Working it Out

Confronting your past is a vital first step in the journey toward self-discovery and inner peace. Until you are ready to do this "inside" work, change cannot occur. Once you are fully open and thoughts begin to flow freely, you will come face to face with some "unfinished business". Some people, for example, may uncover feelings about hurt, pain, fear and death of a parent or caregiver. Feelings of shame about rape or incest, divorce or marriage are uncomfortable and distressing. These painful issues that are not uncovered will continue to poison current relationships.

The Tools To Keep The Focus On Self

I still have support groups, therapists, spiritual advisers and peer counseling to help me see myself and to take an honest look at those parts of me that needed changing. As I meditated, it seemed that deep down inside of me there was a push to seek peace, a new direction, new people, a new way of life. I knew that it was time to let go of the ego view of self, to analyze the good and bad and learn to respect and like myself.

As a result, I have, to the best of my ability, developed a set of exercises which will help you to work through the process of self-discovery and healing. These techniques could be compared to Peeling An Onion; you are urged to keep peeling off layers until the underlying cause is clearly in focus. Keep asking "Why?" and a clear answer will come. Please refer to the "Peeling An Onion" diagram on the following page.

These six steps are designed to give a clear and focused process in being open and honest in a nurturing atmosphere where others can help by sharing their own experiences of the what, why, how and when of their past. Follow these steps to achieve positive results of inner healing, breaking the cycle and learning to take care of oneself.

Here is a brief overview of the six steps to CST:

1. **Joining and engaging:** A relaxed and easygoing open style establishing a therapeutic peer relationship. A good place to start, "What is going on in your life now?"

2. **Information gathering:** Data-collecting. This relaxed friendly atmosphere allows you to share your feelings, fears, successes and failures with an individual or in a group setting. Such an atmosphere allows you to be at home with your feelings. Any information exchanged during this step must be held in confidence.

3. **Identifying and analyzing:** At this point, some subtle changes are experienced within your awareness and consciousness. This is a self-directed learning process in which you must focus on yourself. "What is my problem? How do I see myself changing?" You may face resistance and denial during this stage. You are encouraged to look inward, share your life story - past, present and future. "Who am I: enabler, codependent, alcoholic, caretaker, overeater...?"

4. **Acceptance:** The Common Sense Therapeutic setting is sensitive and supportive, with a holistic approach to health and healing, allowing you to come to grips with self-acceptance and "break free" of old bondage.

5. **Decision-making:** Strategies and goals - what is appropriate in action and direction. The focus is on alternatives or changes in life-styles. "The fear of the Lord is the beginning of wisdom." (Ps. 111:10) We do have choices, we can expand and not limit ourselves. Sometimes, we place unrealistic expectations upon loved ones or individuals who are struggling with their own shame, guilt, fears, hurt and pain.

6. Evaluation: Priority-based short and long term goals. The criteria is established in a goal-setting or decision-making process and should be realistic and attainable. If the counseling is successful, then changes in your behavior should occur.

"Praise the Lord, His mercy endureth forever."
(Ps. 136:1)

As you peel away your layers through "Common Sense Therapy", meditation and prayer you will find your golden inner-self.

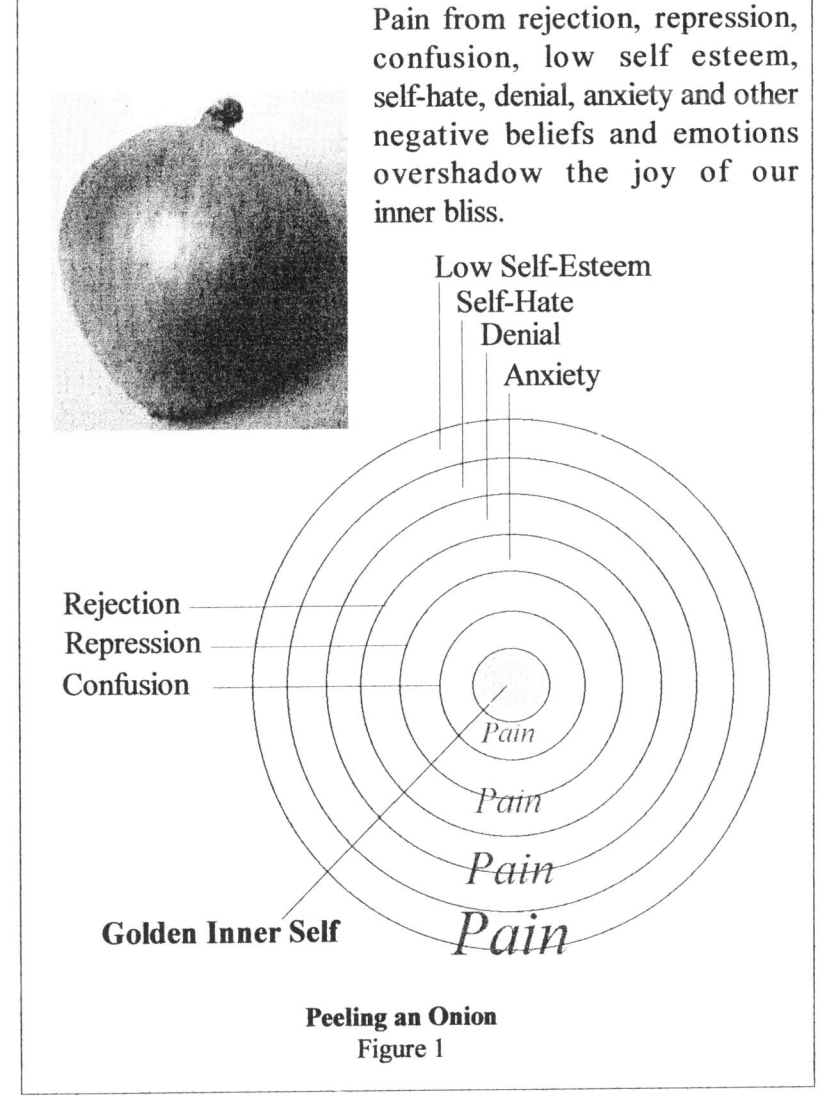

Pain from rejection, repression, confusion, low self esteem, self-hate, denial, anxiety and other negative beliefs and emotions overshadow the joy of our inner bliss.

Low Self-Esteem
Self-Hate
Denial
Anxiety

Rejection
Repression
Confusion

Pain
Pain
Pain
Pain

Golden Inner Self

Peeling an Onion
Figure 1

Please take a moment now to reflect on your reading. Feel free to use this space to make notes, respond to the reading, list ideas or write down tasks you will need to accomplish and to complete this step of the process.

Let the Journey Begin

Step One (1)

Take Three Deep Breaths

Joining and engaging: A relaxed and easygoing process that requires a trusted friend, spiritual advisor or mentor with whom to share your story. The chemistry between the two of you must create an atmosphere of mutuality, trust and respect for the common goal of emotional wellness. No form of confidentiality can or will go forward without the achievement of this first step.

Honest communication is the key to making this process work. This trusted partner should be an active listener and observer, a person with empathy and a genuine care and concern for others. She or he must accept and validate you as you work through specific issues, yet keep an emotional distance. A detached involvement helps to reinforce or fortify the process. Your partner must be able to give you an opportunity to think, to openly express what is going on within and without, get some feedback and to write in a journal to be reviewed at a later time. This is very important for personal growth and self-awareness.

The trusted person shares in your realities and knows that you have a need to be loved, needed and to feel worthwhile. There are lots of risks involved in personal sharing. There is no way around the pain. Spirituality is encouraged throughout the joining and engaging process. You must ask yourself, "How can I let go of the past, without blaming, finger-pointing and self-doubt? What are the benefits?"

Please take a moment now to reflect on your reading. Feel free to use this space to make notes, respond to the reading, list ideas or write down tasks you will need to accomplish and to complete this step of the process.

Step Two (2)

Information gathering: Look into your childhood. What happened, with whom, when and where? How do you feel about this or that? What action was taken on your behalf? The information gathering helps in determining the various assessments of the strengths and weaknesses of your family, culture, community and society at large[1]. Information gathering is an effective tool because it is direct, practical and an honest approach to personal growth and healing.

Information cannot be snatched or forced from someone, but must be given freely. For example, some families are very wary of anyone who tries to force information from them. They have reason to be suspicious of what they perceive as prying into their lives by anyone, even well-meaning peers and therapists. Issues such as out-of-wedlock births, marital status of parents or paternity of the children are family "secrets" that we hesitate to discuss with an outsider.

Some families have legitimate reasons to be weary and suspicious of sharing such information about themselves, for in doing so, it may be devastating to them mentally, emotionally and economically. Though there may be resistance in sharing, all people, no matter what their station in life, need to be valued and validated. Only then can they share their feelings, knowing that the information will not be used against them.

Over the years I resisted change because of fear inside of me. I didn't want to look at my life. I was isolated and had many secrets. I attended church and was also very active in church,

---

[1] Transference and countertransference can be useful methods in reviewing such information.

however, it was not until I got into self-help support groups that I could express my feelings openly and honestly. I spent years feeling sorry for myself, filled with guilt, self pity, low self-esteem, crying, working overtime trying to make my home and family happy. I wanted them to love me.

It didn't happen until I began to get honest and learn to accept me and to understand that I have no control over anyone but me, and the work begins on the inside. I could no longer run away from myself. I had to unlearn many patterns of attitude, and behaviors in-order to let go. I found the key was in sharing my experience, strength and hope to others.

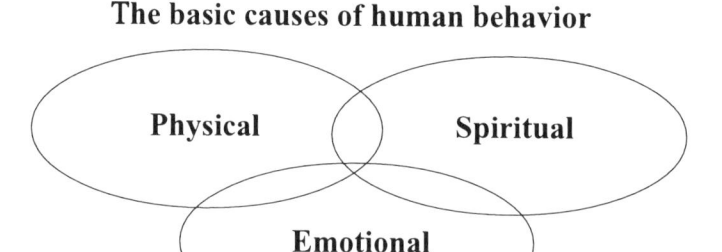

The basic causes of human behavior

- Physical
- Spiritual
- Emotional

Each is impinged upon the other. When some trouble spot is going on within me, at times I question where it is coming from. For example, a headache; I may not have gotten enough sleep, may have overworked or it may have been something else. On the other hand I may not have considered the fact that there were some unresolved emotional conflicts that I needed to deal with.

I think back to my ancestors and grandparents and it seemed that they had a better understanding of human behavior than we do now. The reason being, that we have a pill for every need and are not very interested in the physical, spiritual or emotional needs of what may be the root cause of the headache. Therefore, the problem not only has a physical and emotional basis, but spiritual as well. Since many problems do have a spiritual cause, they also follow with a spiritual solution. This is evident by the number of people seeking counseling, psychological and psychiatric care.

God describes man:
"I will Praise Thee, for I am fearfully and wonderfully made; marvelous are thy works; and that my soul knoweth right well"

(Psalm 139:14)

Please take a moment now to reflect on your reading. Feel free to use this space to make notes, respond to the reading, list ideas or write down tasks you will need to accomplish and to complete this step of the process.

Step Three (3)

Identifying and Analyzing: After a few sessions of CST, thoughts and feelings will appear indicating that a deep awareness is taking place. The basic change has begun. "In quietness and in confidence shall be your strength." (Isaiah 30:15) We all must recognize that it is "I" who must do the work. There will be a calmness, a constructive attitude, in the midst of confusion that is within you. Know that as you identify and analyze the change at the center of your being, there is God.

During my own deepening awareness, it was evident that I had lots of old behavior patterns to work on. As a child, I saw no display of affection in my home, so I was ashamed and uncomfortable to show any in my adult home. Our personal goal is nothing less than the radical restructuring of individual behavior. This <u>restructuring</u> or <u>transformation</u> of individual dysfunctions, inappropriateness and negativism is what **God** can do for **His people. HE DOES NOT** want any of us to be hurt, overwhelmed and defeated by the world in which we live. The Apostle Paul states that **GOD WANTS** us to "...be not conformed to this world; but be ye transformed by the renewing of your mind, that ye may prove what is good and acceptable and perfect will of **GOD**." (Romans 12:2)

I'm glad something positive has come from a more difficult time in my life. So much energy was spent trying to help those who didn't want nor need my help. Today much focus is on how we treat each other especially children. It is believed that many children as well as adults are suffering from some form of depression. The feeling of being unloved, not measuring up, low self-esteem, feeling rejected, not appreciated, unrealistic goals, and physical condition can cause depression. Unless these misconceptions are corrected the patterns of guilt and depression may develop even more serious at a later age.

When such unhealthy patterns are replaced by acceptance, encouragement and praise the symptoms frequently disappear. As we are given the freedom to express our thoughts and feelings, the guilt and fear of these feelings gradually diminish. Spiritual understanding is important in this common sense therapy since it concerns such unacceptable attitudes. As a person grows toward spiritual maturity they (s/he)will do many things which are not desirable, but that God readily forgives. We replace evil thoughts and actions with right thinking and right actions. This spiritual understanding and growth is a vital factor in learning to accept oneself and overcome the tendency to repress, and disassociate certain aspects of one's personality.

View points on mental and emotional disturbances

Parental rejection;
The parent has done many things to make the child feel inadequate
- not enough time with child
- refused to give attention and affection
- lack of love

Overly critical parents;
- criticize child
- show displeasure if child does not measure up
- neglect or overlook child

Cruel parent behavior;
  - rejection, punitive and physically abusive
  - verbally abusive

Unconscious feelings of hostility;
  - strong feeling of worthlessness and feeling no good
  - resent the way parent mistreated her/him as a child
  - have a felt need for punishment

Past traumatic experience;
  - tragic loss of loved one
  - childhood sexual experience
  - conflicts between instinctual drives and demands of society

The drives of sex and hostility are prominent in this orientation. Since these behaviors are unacceptable to society, these feelings must be repressed. As time goes on the individual has a need to satisfy the physiological sex urge to vent feelings of hostility (out of the closet).

Normal experiences an adult faces.
Adjustment difficulties;
  - marital difficulties
  - personality disturbances
  - abusive behavior
  - drinking
  - sexual affairs
  - lack of communication

Never underestimate;
- the power of a smile
- a firm handshake
- a warm greeting

These are tools for positive relationships.

Respect for self and others is important to remember:

Unconditional love has no strings attached.

Detachment

From the third step of CST, it is necessary for you to write down a list of what to do on a daily basis, i.e.., attend meetings, talk to a trusted friend about your pain and success do something for someone outside of the family. The more you immerse yourself in spiritual learning, the more help you will receive from a source greater than yourself. You will soon learn that we are all powerless over other people and their behavior, and that, by turning it over to your higher power, you will gain mastery over yourself.

We do not know <u>how</u> another person feels until we walk in their shoes. They may be unhappy and looking to find something to make them feel better. I learned to concentrate on the solution, not the problem. There are reasons why things happen as they do; someday, we will find out the reason, if it is for us to know.

There are a plethora of ways to identify and analyze data, and find a treatment modality or the appropriate therapeutic intervention* that will be best suited. For example, in dealing with behaviors, such as individual, group, joint or family therapies, multiple family, multiple impact or network therapy, behavior modification, brief therapy or family crisis intervention, make use of videotaping various sessions,

family mapping and family sculpturing in order to work through the various dysfunctions of the past.

Detachment -to disconnect, to disengage, to separate, not involved by emotion. (Webster's New World Dictionary)

These behaviors have a myriad of classifications but very specific definitions: passive-aggressive, aggressive, obsessive, compulsive, compulsive-obsessive, manic, depressive, bipolar affective disorder, etc. Yet, there is still a need to "make it plain", to breakdown this language into a simple form for the so called "layman". It is very important to share what he or she feels are the underlying problems, thus, <u>making a diagnosis</u>. He or she must be able to analyze the patterns and problems that have been both crippling and debilitating over a number of years.

One of the tremendous ways of identifying, analyzing and helping work through patterns and problems is by relabeling or reframing. Relabeling means changing the label or meaning of a word or phrase in order to make dysfunctional behavior reasonable and understandable. For example, referring to alcoholism as a sickness rather than a disease or labeling poor students as educationally different rather than educationally disadvantaged. Changing the language, changing the concept can, indeed, bring about change in the individual.

Please take a moment now to reflect on your reading. Feel free to use this space to make notes, respond to the reading, list ideas or write down tasks you will need to accomplish and to complete this step of the process.

Step Four (4)

Acceptance or Refocusing:

One of the worst feelings any one of us could have is the notion that we do not measure-up, do not belong or that we are not OK. If or when you are subjected to unrealistic expectations, a negative self-concept or being the butt of jokes and innuendo, you are constantly made to feel at odds with yourself. Those of us who have felt overwhelmed, repressed, depressed, defeated and powerless know such feelings very well. No individual, person, ethnic group or child should ever be subjected to this kind of mean-spiritedness and harshness. Again, Some families have become all too familiar with such subjugation from within.

Acceptance

I spent many years trying to be someone else. I'm short and have bowlegs. My friends would call me "shorty" and "duck legs", which I hated. Each time they would call me these names, I would get angry. The turning point came when I accepted myself as I am. I remember hearing myself saying, "Girl, this is it. This is all you got. You will not get any taller and your legs will not get any longer. You better live within and learn to do something with it."

I heard a voice saying, "Turn it over to me. You and I are going to get along just fine and I'll be able to use you just as you are." I had to accept myself as I was. I had to acknowledge and surrender my will to **God**. As I thanked and praised **God** for this experience, I felt that there was no relief, but as I continued to be thankful, very slowly, I felt **God's** presence. I had to accept me!

One of the ways I found acceptance is through refocusing of my self-concept. The <u>Dictionary of Psychology</u> defines self-concept as, "all the elements that make up a person's view of himself, including self-image."[2] Through refocusing, the negative person who feels defeated, overwhelmed, lonely and withdrawn begins to view him or herself differently. His or her self-image changes in a positive way. They look in the mirror and see vibrant, wholesome, worthwhile persons, who believe in themselves. One can change and bring new meaning to their lives and be OK. Perhaps Dr. Thomas Harris, in his book, I'm OK, You're OK[3], sums it up best:

> "We cannot guarantee instant OK feelings by the assuming of the I'M OK, YOU'RE OK position. We have to be sensitive to the presence of the old recordings; but we can choose to turn them off when they replay in a way that undermines the faith we have in a new way to live, which, in time, will bring forth new results and new happiness in our living."

We must learn to reach out to positive others. We must be consistent with our progress. We must continue to peel layers of hurt, resentment and fear to reach out to a power that is greater than ourselves. Each of us can change ourselves, if or when we desire to seek to be sensitive and supportive.

CST offers a holistic approach to healing and health, a new, innovative life-style and the motivation to "break free" of the old bonds.

---

[2] Stratt, David, Dictionary of Psychology, Barnes and Noble, Philadelphia, 1981, p. 111.

[3] Harris, Thomas A., I'm OK - You're OK, Avon Books, New York, 1973, p. 77.

"We shall not all sleep, but we shall be changed, in a moment, in the twinkling of an eye,."

(I Corinthians 15:51-52).

God shall change us all. A line in a church hymn seems very appropriate here. It states, "There is no secret what **God** can do. What **He** has done for others, **He will do** for you".

The deepest craving in human nature is the desire to be appreciated. When was the last time you praised someone or gave a sincere word of appreciation? Set your feelings aside for a moment: **stop, listen, think** and reason why with yourself. Think how the other person feels.

Life is a mirror; like attract like; therefore do the following:

- Praise or admire rather than criticize, condemn or complain
- Show interest in others
- Integrity provides self reliances
- Be flexible
- tactfulness
- always assume there are two sides to every story. Deeds speak louder than words. Build up those around you and never minimize the achievement of others.
- Be humble, meek and bold

Enthusiasm is more than wealth; it is a zest for living and a burning desire. Dr. Martin Luther King says " A street sweeper has lived a great life who did his job well as a street sweeper."

Love comes when we least expect it, and when we are not looking for it. Hunting for love never brings the right partner. It only creates longing and unhappiness.

Love is never outside ourselves; Love is within us.

Love teaches us about building healthy relationships by first getting to know ourself.

Learning the importance of Common Sense by looking at ourselves. We seek to learn what we missed from our childhood; our stubbornness, willfulness, pride, greed, anger. It's my way or no way attitude. Also the joy, empathy, inner peace and knowing that I am never alone.

Role of boundaries

Know how and when to say **NO** to family situations, sex, monetary issues, business, or whatever. As we make common sense and God sense a part of us, we will develop a clearer (picture) of honesty, self-esteem, spirituality and fulfillment. It is a process.

In building a healthy relationship we will only be as successful as the health of the relationship. We may have the best intentions but surrounded with unhealthy people. We need to break the cycle and admit we can't do it alone. We need trusted people to support and give encouragement. We can't run away from ourself. If there is no self examination the same situation will follow with the same results.

On a journey of Self Discovery we have embarked on a spiritual journey to explore our hidden motives, secrets, buried memories and unrecognized talents. We learn to overcome obstacles to personal growth. God's solutions are the only ones that work.

* Interventions- to come in to modify, settle, or hinder some action. Interference in the affairs of another (Webster's New World Dictionary).

Please take a moment now to reflect on your reading. Feel free to use this space to make notes, respond to the reading, list ideas or write down tasks you will need to accomplish and to complete this step of the process.

Step Five (5)

Strategies and Goals:

Decision-making is not an easy task. Many people, specifically adults, <u>struggle most of their lives in this area</u>. It is very scary, risky and uncomfortable, yet a task that must be carried out. Decision-making, like many other things, is a learned behavior. If you have not been either encouraged or exposed to the decision-making process, then it will be very difficult to make appropriate decisions or decisions of any kind without hesitation or "what ifs". The more you are exposed or encouraged to make decisions, the more capable you will become.

One of the ways that decision-making skills can be practiced or become a reality is in the restructuring of individual behavior. Restructuring means changing from one system to another, one pattern to another, one life-style to another. It involves changing the structure and organization within the family, group or individual. The trusted friend shares and teaches a new pattern of behavior and, hopefully, a new life-style.

The creator of restructuring or structural family therapy is the "renowned" Salvador Minuchin. Dr. J. C. Wynn, former professor of family therapy at the Colgate Rochester Divinity School in Rochester, New York, quoted Minuchin's work stating that "structural family therapy is aimed at helping unorganized and dysfunctional families to restructure themselves into better organization with more adequate coping skills.[4] CST attempts to bring about major change in your life-style, as well as with

---

[4] Wynn, Dr. J. C., <u>Family Therapy and Pastoral Ministry</u>, Harper & Rowe, San Francisco, CA, 1982, p. 60

behaviors which could stand in your way of healing and achieving.

During the decision-making process, you choose a goal that is appropriate for yourself. You focus in a decisive way towards an alternative change in your life-style. It is a process that takes time - time to be silent, meditative, to read, to write in your journals, to be thankful and not afraid to acknowledge the presence of God to direct one's life each day.

It is a process that allows you to believe in yourself and strengthen your belief in **God**. It allows you to communicate more openly and honestly, to give your support without expecting anything in return. This is a commitment that you are making to yourself. The next step is to openly tell someone. This helps to keep you honest with yourself, to face your personal fears. This may alter or bring about a change in your relationships. You begin to face problems or concerns. Slowly and subtly, you will know that God is doing for you what you cannot do for yourself.

The issue of personal esteem is so deep and frightening to look at, that most of us will not acknowledge it as a factor when we face the fear of losing a relationship. Doubting our own self-worth is what makes most of us lose faith in our decision. We must remember our relationship is built on love, respect and sharing. Our greatest fears are that, if told the truth, we would no longer have this relationship. It is very important that we deal openly with issues in relationships.

When partners separate without dealing with underlying attitudes and insecurities, they will most likely repeat the same situations with a new partner. It is not the relationship that is the culprit. The problem lies in the deep-seated fears, attitudes, personalities and behavior of the past called emotional baggage, which we carry like a heavy weight from relationship to relationship.

Decision-making is necessary to begin a new life based on realistic expectations. Slight changes in attitude and behavior can make a big difference. CST can help as a source of insight, support and direction in getting started. Anyone who chooses to take the necessary steps will find health and healing leading to a happier and fulfilled life. You will see faith in action.

Please take a moment now to reflect on your reading. Feel free to use this space to make notes, respond to the reading, list ideas or write down tasks you will need to accomplish and to complete this step of the process.

Step Six (6)

Evaluation

Remember, you must keep yourself from care taking. A caretaker or people-pleaser is a person who lets another person's behavior affect him or her and who is obsessed with controlling that person's behavior. It is someone who grew up confusing being needed with being loved. It is someone who neglects or ignores his or her own needs and wishes. In a misguided effort to help, the caretaker deprives family or friends of the motivation to change. Those family members or friends remain the same needy, dependent people with low self-esteem and not the mature adults the caretaker thinks he or she is helping them to become.

Caretakers or people-pleasers learned their unhealthy behavior or were victims of a painful or difficult childhood. They grew up in dysfunctional families where they did not receive effective nurturing. Ceasing to be a caretaker or people-pleaser requires a conscious decision to alter the way one interact with everyone.

As part of the Evaluation process, you should do some or all of the following tasks:

1. Write a note of thanks.
2. Don't do for others if they can or should be doing for themselves.
3. Break your routine behavior by force of your will.
4. Smile often.
5. Treat yourself the same as you treat your best friend.
6. Prioritize the things about yourself that you want to change.
7. Take good care of yourself. Have the appearance of well-

being and happiness.
8. Pray often.
9. Take care how you dress, what you eat, how you look and exercise your physical and spiritual self.
10. Make friends of your own. Join clubs, volunteer, take classes, get a part-time job, get a life of your own.
11. Think of what you have to be grateful for. Make a list in your journal.
12. Make a conscious effort to acknowledge and recognize what is going on within yourself.
13. Learn to compliment others.

We all need help sometimes. We must take time to think before jumping into a situation, when our "help" will prevent someone from learning something he or she needs to know. Looking back, I can see now that the help I thought I was giving to my husband and family only blocked the lessons they needed to learn. I took away their right to solve their own problems. Since I started allowing others to tackle their own problems, I have been surprised how ingenious and resilient they are. So, start now and return all those obligations and duties to their rightful owners, keeping only the ones that belong to you.

> **"Be kind to one another, tenderhearted, forgiving one another, as God in Christ forgave you."**
> Esphesians 4:32

We struggle to be free from anger, fear, resentment and loved ones, only to discover that our bondage doesn't come from outside sources. Where there is life there is hope.

God can restore us to our loving self. We must never allow fear and shame to keep us from approaching **God for forgiveness and healing.** He is **waiting for us to reach out and touch the hem of his garment.**

Attitude

Attitude is your most priceless possession! It enhances careers, improves relationships, fosters good health, improves memory, supports a good sense of humor, promotes relaxation, and enables us to let go of " worn out" relationships.

Reminder:

Self-help, support groups are available through agencies, Churches, Alcoholics Anonymous and others.

Love Lifted Me

Breaking the caretaker game is a real test of Common Sense love. Like charity, love begins at home in the heart. Love is kind and is able to stand back so that others may learn their lesson of life. The love we have for others is directly proportional to the love we have for ourselves. For helping those we love is taking care of ourselves, providing for our own growth and developing our own talents. What is there to learn if we know everything? How does anyone improve on perfection? Are we playing **God** with other people's lives?

We do not need to be hampered by our own insecurities and fears, while it might break our hearts to lose someone. If we can honestly say, "I want you to be all you can with or without me," then we know our love is genuine. Leaving others to work out their own rewards gives them the joy and self-esteem of accepting the consequences of their own feelings and action. We should learn not to carry others, but to walk with them side by side.

As I let go of the old baggage and burdens that I was carrying (comparing, judging, analyzing, blaming, guilt, etc.) I felt so much lighter and brighter, feeling inner peace. My mind is not in turmoil and constantly churning.

Letting go of the old attitudes and rigid belief and behaviors that I had been living with. I am more willing to unmask fears, take risks and respect life on life terms.

---

[5] Smith, Howard E. and James Rowe, "Love Lifted Me", ASCAP, 1912. Taken from The Hymnal for Worship & Celebration, Word Music, Waco, Texas, 1986, p. 505.

I thank my wonderful, talented and independent children for being excellent teachers and mirrors for me. Thanks to my husband—a teacher in his own way, unconditional love, support, acceptance of my need to be me. Thanks for the fun, laughter and enjoyment.

As it is stated in the song:

"Love Lifted Me"[5]

I was sinking deep in sin, far from the peaceful shore,

very deeply stained within, sinking to rise no more.

But the Master of the sea, heard my despairing cry.

From the waters he lifted me.

When nothing else could help, Love Lifted Me.

Please take a moment now to reflect on your reading. Feel free to use this space to make notes, respond to the reading, list ideas or write down tasks you will need to accomplish and to complete this step of the process.

Getting to know Me!

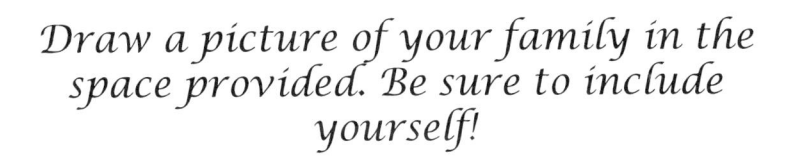

Draw a picture of your family in the space provided. Be sure to include yourself!

Use the facing page if you need additional space.

Exercise 1

Identify and explain the role you play in the drawing.

Exercise 2

Identify and explain the support you receive from: family, friends, community, others.

Exercise 3

Explain how you feel about your family, who or what brings your family together? Who is the center figure in your family?

Exercise 4

Who did you play with as a child? What was your favorite game or pastime?

Exercise 5

What qualities did you like most about your best friend?
Explain:

What qualities did you like least about your best friend?
Explain:

Exercise 6

What was the most important event that happened to you during the last three (3) years?
Explain:

Exercise 7

What are your goals for the next six months Explain:

For the next year:

For the next 3 years:

Exercise 8

What actions are you taking on a daily basis to make your goals come true?
Explain:

Exercise 9

What activities do you engage in for fun and relaxation?
Explain:

Exercise 10

Who do you treat better your self or your best friend?
Explain:

Suggested Reading:

Bloomfield, Harold, Making Peace With Your Parents, Ballantine, New York, 1983

Engel, Beverly, Emotionally Abused Women: Overcoming Destructive Patterns and Reclaiming Yourself, Fawcett-Columbine, New York, 1988

Fairchild Dictionary of Sociology, RGA Publishing Group, Inc., New York, 1990

Forward, Susan and John Torres, Men Who Hate Women and The Women Who Love Them, Bantam, New York, 1986

Giordano, John, et al., eds., Ethnicity and Family Therapy, The Guilford Press, New York, 1982

Goldenberg, Herbert and Irene Goldenberg, Family Therapy: An Overview, Brooks-Cole, Montrey, CA, 1980

Gordon, Richard, The Healing Hands, The Polarity Experience, Unity Press, Santa Cruz, CA, 1978

Harris, Thomas A., I'm OK - You're OK, Avon Books, New York, 1973

Hollies, Linda, Inner Healing for Broken Vessels: Seven Steps to Mending Childhood Wounds, Woman to Woman Ministries, Inc. Publications, Joliet, IL, 1991

Miller, Alice, For Your Own Good: Hidden Cruelty in Child-Rearing and the Roots of Violence, Farrar, Straus, Giroux, New York, 1984

Nakken, Craig, The Addictive Personality: Understanding

Peck, M. Scott, The Road Less Traveled, Simon & Schuster, New York, 1978

Smith, Howard E. and James Rowe, "Love Lifted Me", ASCAP, 1912. Taken from The Hymnal for Worship & Celebration, Word Music, Waco, Texas, 1986, p. 505.

Statt, David, Dictionary of Psychology, Barnes & Noble, Philadelphia, 1981

The Holy Bible

Vanant, Iyanla, Tapping the Power Within: A Path to Self-Empowerment for Black Women, Harlem River Press, New York, London, 1992

White, Evelyn C., The Black Women's Health Book: Speaking for Ourselves, The Seal Press, Seattle, WA, 1990

Whitfield, Charles, Healing the Child Within: Discovery and Recovery for Adult Children of Dysfunctional Families, Health Communications, Pompano Beach, FL, 1987

Woititz, Janet, Adult Children of Alcoholics, Health Communications, Inc., Hollywood, FL, 1983

Word Music, The Hymnal for Worship & Celebration, Word Music, Waco, Texas, 1986

Wynn, Dr. J. C., Family Therapy and Pastoral Ministry, Harper & Rowe, San Francisco, CA, 1982

Compulsion In Our Lives, Harper & Row, San Francisco, 1988

Seminars with Jessie James

At a time when we need solutions to the myriad of problems we have in life, Jessie James Seminars provide an opportunity to identify areas within our relationships to create a safe and supportive environment to explore these issues.

Seminars are open to anyone who wishes to experience a journey of honesty, self-esteem, spirituality and fulfillment using common sense techniques that promote love.

Topics for discussion

— healing power of self-esteem

— sharing, honesty, open-mindedness and willingness

— nurturing male/female relationships

— effective ways to establish communications

— learning to love oneself

— develop positive self-esteem by acknowledging past experiences and giving yourself permission to create the life you want.

These seminars/workshops and lectures will inspire and motivate you to reap the rewards you deserve and love yourself more in the process.

Jessie M. James, B.A., M.A.

Jessie is a native of Sanford, Florida, who came to Rochester in 1952. She is married, the mother of four grown children and has four grandchildren.

During her tenure at the Rochester Institute of Technology, Jessie was a Program Administrator and faculty member in the College of Continuing Education. Her responsibilities included program development, financial management and implementation of training, seminars and conferences, hiring instructors, marketing and counseling.

Jessie has authored numerous articles and reports on community affairs and social changes. She has received many awards expressing appreciation for her leadership. She has an enviable record of community service. She is a counselor, confidant, a woman with a vision. Jessie is an outstanding, enlightened woman, ready to inspire others, using her Common Sense Therapy and sense of humor.

She continues to travel extensively across the country, giving lectures, participating in conferences, seminars, workshops and training in self-development, personal relationships and leadership skills. A worldwide traveler, Jessie's warm smile and inner strengths have won her respect from people from all walks of life.

In 1987, Mrs. James organized the "Jessie James Is Cruising Again" campaign to encourage people to travel and learn to take care of themselves, which she continues to do each year during the second week of July. For eight years, she had the "Jessie James Hideaway" for college students to provide a home away from home, while maintaining an active private training and consulting practice.

It is helpful that Jessie is a bundle of energy. Locomotives run out of steam, cars run out of gas, but Jessie's energy seems endless. She gets a refill from a supply many of us fail to use. Her energy is faith, her filling station is God!

Her local volunteer activities include membership in the Aenon Baptist Church, American Association for Adult and Continuing Education and Toastmaster's Club, as well as board membership with the John F. Wegman Fund and the Anthony L. Jordan Foundation.

Jessie's credentials include a diploma in Leadership Training and Development from RIT, a certificate in Leadership Training and Self-Awareness from the Gabriel Richard Institute, a diploma in Drug Dependence Training from Yale University, certificates in Motivation and Human Values from the Presbyterian Institute and a Certificate of Ordination, Short Courses, at the Colgate Divinity School in Rochester, NY.

"Where there is no vision, the people perish."

Watch for the next Jessie M. James book:

This Is My Story this is My Song

To contact Jessie to ask for advice, to make an appointment, schedule a workshop or lecture, or just to say hello.

Write to: Jessie M. James
at: HAPPE Programs, Inc.
            183 Saint Paul Street
            Rochester, New York 14604

To order additional books, inquire about other books Jessie has written or to request a free catalogue of evolutionary products and programs call:

1-800-RU-HAPPE or 1-800-784-2773